10 HABITS OF EFFECTIVE COMPLIANCE PROFESSIONALS

Dilip Jain

Made with ♥ on the Notion Press Platform
www.notionpress.com

Disclaimer

This book is intended for educational and informational purposes only. The views and opinions expressed herein are those of the author and do not necessarily reflect the official policy or position of any agency, organization, employer, or company. The content is provided "as is," and the author makes no representations or warranties of any kind concerning the accuracy, completeness, suitability, or validity of any information contained herein. Any reliance you place on such information is strictly at your own risk.

All names, characters, businesses, places, events, and incidents in this book are either the product of the author's imagination or used in a fictitious manner. Any resemblance to actual persons, living or dead, or actual events is purely coincidental. The scenarios and dialogues presented are entirely fictional and are designed solely to illustrate the concepts discussed.

The author and publisher shall not be liable for any loss or damage arising directly or indirectly from the use of the information contained in this book. Readers are encouraged to consult with appropriate professionals for specific advice tailored to their situation.

In the ever-evolving landscape of financial compliance, professionals are continually challenged to adapt to new regulations, technologies, and ethical considerations. This book introduces a novel approach by distilling the essence of effective compliance into "**The 10 Habits of Effective Compliance Professionals.**" Through engaging narratives and practical scenarios, it offers readers a comprehensive guide to mastering these essential habits.

The genesis of this work stems from a recognition that, while technical knowledge is vital, the cultivation of specific habits can significantly enhance a compliance professional's effectiveness. By embedding these habits into daily practice, professionals can navigate complexities with greater agility and foresight.

To bring these concepts to life, the book employs a cast of fictional characters—Aisha, Ravi, Lena, and Omar—each representing diverse roles within the compliance ecosystem. Their interactions and experiences provide relatable insights into the practical application of the 10 habits, bridging the gap between theory and real-world practice.

This work aims not only to inform but also to inspire a proactive and principled approach to compliance. By internalizing these habits, professionals can contribute to fostering a culture of integrity and accountability within their organizations.

Note: All names and characters depicted in this book are entirely fictitious. Any resemblance to real persons, living or dead, is purely coincidental. This material is intended for educational purposes only.

Best Wishes

Dilip Jain

Acknowledgements

Writing this book has been a journey shaped by countless conversations, shared experiences, and the encouragement of a professional community that believes in the power of ethical, proactive, and human-centered compliance.

First and foremost, I extend my heartfelt gratitude to the compliance professionals—both new and seasoned—who inspired this work. Your dedication to navigating complex regulatory landscapes while upholding integrity is what makes our field not just relevant, but indispensable.

To my mentors and peers in the financial services and regulatory space: thank you for your insights, your challenges, and your support. You have helped refine not just this book, but my own understanding of what it means to be truly effective in compliance.

A special thank you to the anonymous voices and real-world case studies that inspired the fictional characters in this book. While their names and stories are imagined, their spirit is very much real—drawn from the trenches of boardrooms, compliance reviews, risk assessments, and regulatory engagements.

To my family and loved ones, your unwavering belief in my work gave me the space to think, write, and create. This book would not exist without your patience and encouragement.

Finally, every reader who picks up this book in pursuit of compliance not just correctly, but meaningfully—this is for you.

With gratitude,

Dilip Jain Dilipjainbooks@gmail.com

About the Author:

CA Dilip Jain has multi-faceted financial experience over his 20 years of banking and financial services career with Kotak Bank, ICICI Bank in India, Daiwa Capital Markets, Bahrain, Daiwa Capital in DIFC, Dubai, Nimai, Crowe Vistra, Oasis Investment Co., Century Private Wealth Ltd, DIFC. His experience spans from lease and hire purchase, asset securitization, indirect tax planning, credit- mortgages, AML risk, compliance, anti-money laundering, trade and corporate finance solutions.

He was the compliance officer for DFSA regulated firms (Category 3C and 4) having diverse business in wealth and asset management, payment services, advisory and arranging services. He was a faculty trainer at ICAI GMCS as well as part of Core ICAI VAT trainer faculty.

As a Qualified Chartered and Cost Accountant, he is also a Certified Anti-Money Laundering Specialist (ACAMS). He has done his executive management development program in 2011 from IIM-Ahmedabad. He is also level 3 certified Risk in financial Services, Securities and Global Financial Compliance, DIFC and UAE rules and regulations, Combating Financial Crime from CISI. He has more than 1000 hours of research and learning experience in AML, compliance and Risk space.

He also led knowledge sessions UAE AML and VAT law implementation and has complied books on Customs, VAT, ESR Corporate Tax and AML laws.

He is also an active Toastmaster, have reached its highest level as Distinguished toastmasters and have undertaken many youth leadership programs and speech craft. He also set Guinness record for world largest memory Game. In his free time, he likes to travel, enjoys early morning walk, read books, and network. He is an active member of ICAI Dubai chapter, Jito International and was past Area Director, Toastmasters International in Dubai. He was featured in Khaleej Times in the UAE Year of Giving for his contribution to community, has featured in "Pearls of Rajasthan" as well as in Nelson Mandela Inspired "Good Deeds" Book, Abu Dhabi.

Other Books By same Author:

1. AML Brain GYM
2. AML brain GYM – For DNFBPs
3. Decoding Corporate Governance
4. 360 Compliance for beginners
5. Case Studies on UAE Corporate Tax (Joint initiative)
6. Case Studies on UAE Transfer Pricing (Joint initiative)
7. Cooked Up Balance Sheet- How to Decode them.
8. Biz Bytes-Know your customer's business.
9. Practicing sustainability- personal stories
10. AML- questions challenge
11. AI for AML
12. Chat GPT for Beginners
13. FATF 40 recommendations simplified
14. CFD firm- AML and Compliance Framework

Other earlier Compilations by same Author:

1. UAE Vat law
2. UAE Corporate Tax Law
3. UAE Economic Substance Regulations
4. UAE AML provisions for DNFBPs
5. UAE Customs Law
6. Zidd Aage Badhne Ke (determined to move ahead)
7. Our story, our Values

"We don't need compliance to slow us down."

That's what the product head said in the strategy meeting.

And just like that, Maya—the newly appointed Head of Compliance—felt the chill of being the outsider in the room. She'd spent three weeks reviewing the product roadmap, aligning it with local regulations, and preparing a risk matrix that she thought would help the business. But now, all eyes were on her, expecting her to either nod along or throw up roadblocks.

She took a breath and replied:

"What if I could help you go faster—but safely?"

The room went silent. Then someone smiled. The conversation shifted. Compliance was no longer a 'brake pedal,' but a seatbelt that let the business drive faster with confidence.

This book is about becoming that kind of compliance professional, the kind who isn't just in the room but drives real impact in it.

Why This Book, and Why Now?

The role of compliance has evolved. Once perceived as box-checking, policy-pushing, and fire-fighting, compliance today is expected to:

- Anticipate risks before they become scandals
- Embed itself into business processes without stalling innovation
- Balance local laws, global standards, and ethical dilemmas
- Influence cultures, not just controls
- And in many cases, be the last line of defense against reputational ruin

This book isn't about rules. It's about habits.

Because effective compliance is more than knowing laws about how you think, act, collaborate, and lead. Laws change, tools upgrade, crises shift—but your habits as a professional shape how well you adapt and influence in any environment.

The *10 Habits of Effective Compliance Professionals* are designed to help you thrive in the dynamic, high-stakes world of compliance.

Who Is This Book For?

- **New compliance officers** who want to build confidence and credibility fast
- **Experienced professionals** looking to reflect, recharge, and retool their approach
- **Business leaders and board members** who want to understand what great compliance looks like
- **Students and career-switchers** considering a future in this critical profession

These habits are universal. Because they're not based on a specific regulation or industry—they're based on what makes people *effective* in this line of work.

What You'll Find Inside

Each of the 10 habits is a chapter, structured like this:

- A relatable story from the trenches of compliance
- The principle explained in plain, practical terms
- Strategies and tools for implementation
- Common challenges (and how to overcome them)
- Reflection questions and action steps
- Self-assessment tool to track your progress

You'll meet recurring fictional professionals—Maya, Aisha, Ravi, Lena, Omar—facing the same dilemmas you do. You'll sit in their meetings, join their struggles, and watch them grow. Their journeys are based on real-world scenarios drawn from hundreds of conversations with compliance leaders.

A Word on Style

This isn't a legal textbook or a compliance manual. It's more like a conversation over coffee with someone who's walked the path—and made the mistakes—before you. It's designed to be thoughtful, occasionally funny, and always useful. There are side bars for quick tips, tools you can photocopy or adapt, and questions that nudge you to reflect deeper.

This is your book. Write in the margins. Use it with your team. Come back to it when you hit a wall or need inspiration.

In the dynamic world of financial compliance, four professionals from diverse backgrounds frequently intersect, each bringing unique perspectives and expertise to the table:

Ravi: A seasoned Money Laundering Reporting Officer (MLRO) at a well-established legacy institution, Ravi possesses a wealth of experience in traditional banking compliance. His deep understanding of regulatory frameworks and risk management makes him a valuable mentor and authority in the field.

Lena: A tech-savvy RegTech consultant, Lena specializes in integrating regulatory technology solutions to streamline compliance processes. Her innovative strategies and knowledge of cutting-edge technologies enable financial institutions to enhance efficiency and accuracy in meeting regulatory requirements.

Omar: A pragmatic regulator known for his practical mindset; Omar focuses on balancing stringent regulatory standards with the operational realities of financial institutions. His approachable demeanor and emphasis on collaboration foster constructive relationships between regulators and the industry.

These characters often engage in dialogues and collaborative efforts, each contributing their unique insights to address the evolving challenges in financial compliance.

Why Habits Matter More Than Rules

Anyone can memorize laws. But what makes a *great* compliance professional isn't knowledge alone, its character, courage, communication, curiosity, and the ability to bring people together.

That's what this book will help you build.

Let's start the journey.

Habit 1: Be Proactive- Manage Risks Before They Manage You

The Story: A Data Breach That Was Waiting to Happen

It wasn't the first time Arjun had warned them. But this time, it was too late.

The call came in on a quiet Thursday morning. A junior analyst in IT was panicking—confidential customer data had been exposed. Someone had clicked a phishing email, and malware had found its way into the internal systems. Sensitive information had been exfiltrated—names, contact details, even ID numbers.

Within minutes, Legal, Compliance, Risk, and IT were pulled into a virtual war room.

And there was Arjun, the firm's Compliance Risk Manager, sitting with his laptop open and a folder marked *"Risk Register – Unresolved Gaps."*

"Exactly this scenario was raised six months ago," he said quietly. "Unpatched software, lack of phishing training, absence of a breach response plan."

The CEO stared in disbelief. *"Why didn't we act on this?"*

Everyone looked at each other. Budget constraints. Too many priorities. Lack of urgency.

But the truth was simpler: **reactive compliance** had become the norm.

💬 The Principle: Proactivity is the First Line of Defense

In the world of compliance, being reactive means cleaning up after messes. Being proactive means preventing them altogether.

Reactive compliance is what happens when a policy is drafted *after* a violation, when training is rushed *after* an inspection, and when controls are installed *after* a scandal.

Proactive compliance, on the other hand, is built on anticipation. It's the habit of scanning the horizon for risks, asking *"What could go wrong?"* and acting before the fire starts.

In many ways, **being proactive is a mindset**—not a function of your title or your budget. It's the decision to lead rather than chase, to inform rather than react.

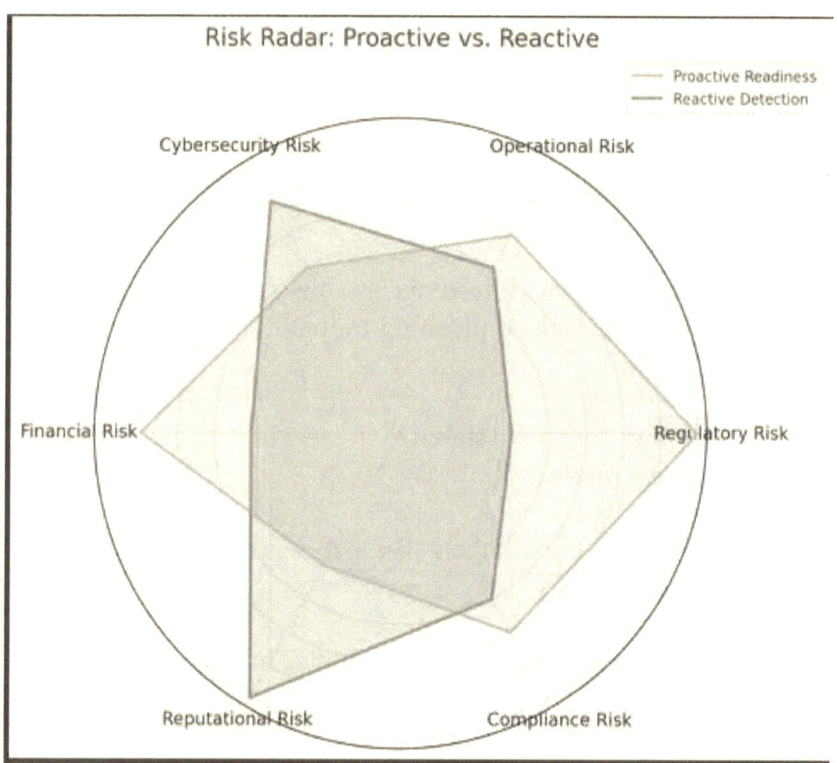

🛠️ Practical Strategies to Build This Habit

☑ 1. Create a Living Risk Register

- Don't let it be a static document. Update it quarterly.
- Include *residual risks*—not just the ones already mitigated.
- Assign ownership for each risk item with follow-up dates.

☑ 2. Conduct Scenario-Based Risk Assessments

- Run simulations. What if there's a cyberattack? A whistleblower case?
- Use tabletop exercises with key departments.

☑ 3. Engage the First Line Early

- Don't wait for issues to escalate up the chain.

- Build informal risk awareness channels (e.g., "Risk Champions" in each team).

✅ 4. Introduce Early-Warning Dashboards

- Use data: compliance exceptions, overdue training, system alerts.
- A spike in minor incidents is often a warning of a major event.

✅ 5. Building a 'Risk Radar' Culture

- Set 15 minutes each month in team meetings for "emerging risks."
- Encourage team members to bring examples from news, competitors, or regulators.

⚠ Common Challenges—and How to Overcome Them

Challenge	Solution
Management doesn't act on early warnings	Present risks in business-impact terms: cost, downtime, reputation.
Risk register is ignored	Tie risk ownership to KPIs or performance reviews.
Too many risks to manage	Use a heat map: focus on high-impact, high-likelihood risks first.
Teams get desensitized to risk	Refresh risk scenarios and rotate stakeholders in assessments.

Dialogue: Maya & Omar Discuss a Silent Threat

Maya (Compliance Officer): "We flagged this KYC backlog three months ago. It's still not cleared."

Omar (Head of Ops): "I know. But no one's raised a serious issue yet. We've been lucky."

Maya: "We won't be lucky forever. Imagine a regulator walks in tomorrow and pulls those files."

Omar: *(pauses)* "So, what's your recommendation?"

Maya: "Let's frame this as an operational continuity risk, not just a compliance risk. I can work with you to estimate the business disruption cost if those accounts are frozen."

Omar: "Now you're speaking my language. Let's get it done."

Quick Tips (Sidebar)

- Use headlines from real enforcement cases to start team discussions.

- Track "near misses" — they're goldmines of learning.

- Have a "Top 5 Risk List" pinned on your department's notice board or dashboard.

- Turn risk reports into infographics — get visibility beyond just the compliance team.

Reflection Questions

1. Do I currently spend more time reacting to issues than preventing them?

2. What risks am I aware of that haven't been escalated or addressed yet?

3. How often do I proactively engage with other departments about risk?

4. What data am I using (or not using) to anticipate risks?

📋 **Action Steps**

- Identify 3 top unresolved risks in your business today.

- Schedule a cross-departmental risk scenario session this month.

- Create a one-page "Risk Alert" template for fast communication.

- Commit to reviewing your risk register every quarter — and making it a discussion document.

- ## Self-Assessment Tool

Statement	Never	Sometimes	Often	Always
I initiate risk assessments even when not prompted	☐	☐	☐	☐
I use real-life examples to explain potential compliance risks	☐	☐	☐	☐
I maintain a dynamic risk register	☐	☐	☐	☐
I convert abstract risks into business-relevant language	☐	☐	☐	☐
I collaborate with other departments to anticipate emerging risks	☐	☐	☐	☐

Tip: A total score below 12? Time to sharpen your proactivity muscle.

Always=4, Never=1

Habit 2: Begin with Compliance by Design

Because Compliance Shouldn't Be an Afterthought

The Story: The Fintech That Launched Too Fast

Aisha was excited. She had just joined a fast-growing fintech startup as their first full-time compliance officer. Day one on the job, she was handed a launch schedule for a new peer-to-peer payment product. The marketing campaign was already live. Influencers were tweeting. Developers were coding at full throttle.

There was just one problem.

No one had reviewed whether the new product complied with local financial promotion regulations—or whether the platform's onboarding met KYC requirements.

Aisha flagged the issues. She raised concerns about onboarding flow, customer data storage, and the product's risk of misuse. But the Product Manager brushed her off: *"Can we patch this later? We need to go live this Friday."*

Aisha watched the team push ahead. And two weeks later, a regulatory notice landed in the CEO's inbox. The firm had breached digital payments guidelines and now faced a formal investigation.

The irony? Fixing the compliance issues *after the fact* took 6x more time, money, and effort than building them in from the start.

The Principle: Build Compliance into the Blueprint

Just as architects plan for fire exits and structural integrity before construction begins, compliance must be embedded at the *design stage*—not tacked on after.

This is the heart of *Compliance by Design*.

It's the habit of sitting at the planning table from day one—whether it's a new product, process, campaign, or system. When compliance is built in from the start, it not only prevents violations but enables smarter, faster execution.

Think of Compliance by Design as:

- Being *preventive*, not corrective

- Supporting *agile*, not obstruction

- Promoting *innovation*, not inhibition

It doesn't mean saying "no" to everything. It means knowing *when and how to say yes—safely.*

Practical Strategies to Build This Habit

1. Insert Compliance into the Project Lifecycle

- Make compliance a mandatory checkpoint in product/project management tools (e.g., JIRA, Asana).

- Create a "Go/No-Go" compliance review checklist.

2. Build Cross-Functional Design Squads

- Embed compliance leads in innovation pods or squads.

- Conduct "Compliance Impact Assessments" alongside technical feasibility studies.

3. Creating a Compliance Design Toolkit

- Templates: KYC flows, disclosure language, data protection impact assessments.

- Pre-approved checklists: marketing reviews, onboarding workflows, vendor due diligence.

4. Schedule Pre-Launch Compliance Reviews

- Don't wait for the final product. Review at wireframe, prototype, and test stages.

- Use "compliance sprints" in agile development cycles.

5. Train Product Teams in Regulatory Thinking

- Teach teams how to spot red flags.

- Use storytelling from real enforcement cases to make it relatable.

⚠ Common Challenges—and How to Overcome Them

Challenge	Solution
Compliance is seen as slowing down innovation	Frame compliance as a competitive differentiator (trust = value).
Compliance isn't invited early in product discussions	Request formal inclusion in project kickoff meetings.
Business speaks "agile," compliance speaks "legalese"	Build shared language—visual risk maps, use cases, checklists.
Compliance teams lack product/tech context	Conduct compliance walkthroughs with product/engineering teams.

Dialogue: Lena & Ravi Debate Product Reviews

Lena (Product Compliance Consultant): "Why don't you review our product roadmap before we build, rather than after?"

Ravi (Senior Compliance Officer): "Because we're not always looped in early enough."

Lena: "Then make yourself essential. Offer value. Show how you can save time and prevent rework."

Ravi: "Fair point. What if I create a product compliance 'starter pack' for your team?"

Lena: "Now we're talking."

🔖 Quick Tips

- Run a 15-minute "Compliance First Aid" for every product team monthly.

- Translate policies into storyboards—showing how requirements apply in real-world flows.

- Add "Compliance Review" to every product launch checklist.

- Use visual traffic-light indicators for faster go/no-go decisions.

❄ Reflection Questions

1. Do I typically get involved early in new product or project discussions?

2. How often do business teams *seek out* compliance proactively?

3. What can I do to make compliance easier to understand for non-legal teams?

4. Are my current review processes preventive or reactive?

✅ Action Steps

- Identify 1–2 upcoming business initiatives and request early involvement.

- Develop a one-page Compliance Design Guide for business/product teams.

- Conduct a retrospective on the last compliance issue, could it have been prevented with early input?

- Propose a "compliance checkpoint" in your organization's project or product lifecycle.

Self-Assessment Tool

Statement	Never	Sometimes	Often	Always
I am involved early in the planning stages of new initiatives	☐	☐	☐	☐
I provide tools/templates that make compliance easier for business	☐	☐	☐	☐
I translate compliance into operational language for teams	☐	☐	☐	☐
I advocate for compliance as a value-creator, not just a guardrail	☐	☐	☐	☐
I help the business understand how compliance supports innovation	☐	☐	☐	☐

Tip: Score yourself again in 90 days. Have you moved from "Sometimes" to "Often" or "Always"?

Habit 3: Put First Things First

Prioritizing Critical Regulatory Requirements

Compliance Priorities Matrix
(Urgent vs. Important)

Urgent & Important	Not Urgent but Important
• Regulatory Audit • Incident Reporting	• Policy Development • Training Programs
• Email Alerts • Quick Fixes	• Low-risk Reviews • Legacy Docs
Urgent but Not Important	**Neither Urgent nor Important**

The Story: Drowning in Compliance, Missing What Matters

Ravi stared at his inbox, feeling overwhelmed.

It was Monday morning, and the compliance team at his mid-sized investment firm had received yet another circular from the regulator, this one about updated cyber reporting timelines. Meanwhile, they were still trying to finalize last quarter's AML report, respond to two due diligence requests from counterparties, update their data privacy policy, and train frontline staff on the latest insider trading restrictions.

The team was doing everything.

Except the one thing that now had the regulator's full attention.

During a recent thematic review, the regulator had flagged several institutions for inadequate Suspicious Transaction Reporting (STR) escalation protocols. Ravi's firm had weak internal documentation on STRs, inconsistent thresholds, and had missed updating procedures in line with new AML guidance.

In the chaos of keeping up with everything, **they missed the one thing they should've been laser-focused on**.

◆ The Principle: Not Everything That Screams is Important

In compliance, everything *feels* important. But not everything *is* equally important.

There's a difference between *urgent* and *critical*. Between what's *loud* and what's *high-risk*.

Effective compliance professionals know how to prioritize. They understand that focusing energy on high-impact, high-risk areas delivers more protection than trying to be perfect in all directions.

This habit is about **regulatory triage** to distinguish:

- What must be done *now*
- What can be scheduled for *later*
- And what can be simplified, delegated, or paused altogether

✖ Practical Strategies to Build This Habit

⊙ 1. Use a Compliance Prioritization Matrix

Plot all obligations by:

- **Impact** (penalty/reputation/business disruption if failed)
- **Probability** (likelihood of occurrence or regulator attention)

Focus on high-impact, high-probability items first.

⊞ 2. Create a Regulatory Obligation Tracker

- Maintain a central tracker with frequency, deadlines, and ownership
- Tag each obligation as critical/core/low (e.g., C1, C2, C3)

3. Align Compliance with Enterprise Risk Appetite

- Ask: "Which obligations align with the business's stated risk appetite?"
- Match your priorities with senior management's risk dashboard

▓ 4. Monitor Regulatory Focus Areas

- Watch enforcement trends, regulator speeches, thematic reviews
- Build a "Regulatory Radar" document reviewed monthly

👥 5. Schedule a Weekly 'Top 3' Alignment Meeting

- Meet with your compliance team or key stakeholders
- Identify the top 3 priorities for the week—and eliminate non-essentials

⚠ Common Challenges—and How to Overcome Them

Challenge	Solution
Everything feels urgent	Use a clear prioritization tool—matrix, scoring, tiering
Lack of clear ownership	Assign compliance leads to each regulation or requirement
Management overloads compliance with low-value tasks	Show the opportunity cost and missed risk coverage
Struggling to say "no" to internal requests	Offer alternatives or defer, but protect core priorities

Dialogue: Aisha & Omar Negotiate Compliance Deadlines

Aisha (Compliance Officer): "I understand this new social media policy is a concern, but our STR framework is overdue for review—and flagged by the regulator."

Omar (Head of Marketing): "But we're going live with our campaign tomorrow."

Aisha: "I can support you with the bare minimum now and schedule a full review next week. But if we neglect STRs, we risk audit findings—or worse, enforcement."

Omar: *(sighs)* "Okay, I get it. STRs first. Let's circle back on social next week."

Quick Tips

- Highlight "Top 5 Compliance Priorities" monthly in your Board report
- Tag every task in your workflow tool by impact level
- Build a "Compliance Calendar" with critical deadlines and checkpoints
- Use "Regulator Lens" — ask: *What would the regulator care about most if they walked in today?*

Reflection Questions

1. Do I have a clear, written list of our top 5 compliance priorities this quarter?
2. How much of my team's time is spent on low-impact or repetitive tasks?
3. Am I using data to guide compliance prioritization?
4. What regulatory areas have the highest consequence if failed?

Action Steps

- Audit your current compliance activities—classify by impact and urgency.
- Build a Top 10 Regulatory Obligations List for your firm and share it with management.
- Introduce a weekly "Compliance Priority Huddle" to align focus.
- Develop a heat map to visualize where attention is most needed.

Self-Assessment Tool

Statement	Never	Sometimes	Often	Always
I maintain a prioritized list of critical compliance requirements	☐	☐	☐	☐
I use risk and impact to decide what gets my attention	☐	☐	☐	☐
I align compliance priorities with the organization's risk appetite	☐	☐	☐	☐
I push back on low-priority distractions to protect focus	☐	☐	☐	☐
I actively monitor regulatory focus areas and adapt priorities	☐	☐	☐	☐

Tip: If your score is below 12, you may be reacting more than prioritizing. Time to reset. Always = 4, Never = 1.

Aligning Compliance with Business Goals

❋ The Story: The Officer Who Always Said "No"

In her early days as a compliance manager at a global logistics firm, Priya was known by one nickname: **"The Gatekeeper."** If anyone came to her with a marketing idea, a product tweak, or a new client onboarding request, they braced for resistance.

"No, this violates policy."
"No, we'll need six weeks for due diligence."
"No, the regulator may not like this."

The business teams saw compliance as the department of "No." Eventually, they stopped coming to her altogether—*until things went wrong*. And when they did, they blamed compliance for not being "solutions-oriented."

It wasn't until her mentor said something that changed her perspective forever:
"Your job isn't to say no." Your job is to say how."

That became her mantra.

She began asking business units what they were trying to achieve. She mapped compliance solutions that still protected the firm but enabled smarter execution. Instead of resisting new ideas, she collaborated early, set guardrails, and even helped teams *accelerate* approvals by creating pre-approved structures.

Six months later, she wasn't "The Gatekeeper" anymore. She was **"The Navigator."**

🤝 The Principle: It's Not Compliance vs. Business—It's Compliance *with* Business

Too often, compliance is seen as an obstacle to growth. But that's a false dichotomy.

Great compliance professionals don't see a zero-sum game between regulation and business goals. They understand that **sustainable success only happens when compliance and business work in harmony**.

Thinking win-win means:

- Understanding what business values

- Finding creative ways to achieve objectives without compromising on integrity
- Being transparent about risks, but also about solutions

Win-win compliance isn't about lowering standards. It's about raising the level of dialogue and trust.

🛠️ Practical Strategies to Build This Habit

❄️ 1. Understand Business KPIs

- Learn what metrics drive decisions (growth, margins, retention, etc.)
- Frame your compliance input in terms of impact on those KPIs

💬 2. Use Risk-Based Flexibility

- Apply proportionality—what's low-risk may need lighter controls
- Propose risk-mitigated alternatives, not just rule citations

🤝 3. Co-Design Solutions

- Set up cross-functional design sessions with business, tech, and ops
- Create "compliance playbooks" that streamline recurring activities

🗣️ 4. Speak Their Language

- Replace legalese with business-relevant phrasing
- Use "If-Then" frameworks: *"If we do X, then Y risk increases—unless we do Z."*

🎯 5. Celebrate Joint Wins

- Recognize teams that partnered well with compliance
- Share stories internally of how compliance enabled success

⚠ Common Challenges—and How to Overcome Them

Challenge	Solution
Business sees compliance as obstructive	Reframe compliance as a risk-management *partner*, not a hurdle
Compliance fears losing independence	Influence through frameworks, not friendliness
Misalignment on timelines or priorities	Use shared planning calendars, prioritization matrices
Business pushes for shortcuts	Offer phased approaches or sandbox pilots with strict boundaries

💬 Dialogue: Ravi & Lena Discuss a High-Risk Client

Ravi (MLRO): "We should reject this client. Too many red flags."

Lena (Head of Sales): "But they're our biggest potential account this year!"

Ravi: "I understand. What if we onboard them under enhanced due diligence, restrict transaction types, and monitor every 30 days?"

Lena: "You'd support it with that framework in place?"

Ravi: "Yes, if we clearly document the controls and the business signs off on shared accountability."

Lena: *(nodding)* "Now that's a win-win."

💡 Quick Tips

- Create a "Compliance with Business Lens" slide for each initiative
- Use analogies—e.g., "Compliance is the seatbelt, not the brake"

- Propose pilot programs to test new ideas under controlled conditions
- Invite business leaders to co-own compliance metrics

Reflection Questions

1. When was the last time I helped a business team *achieve* a goal compliantly?
2. Do I regularly sit in on commercial or product strategy meetings?
3. Have I asked business leaders how they perceive compliance?
4. What controls or processes could I simplify without increasing risk?

Action Steps

- Set up monthly alignment meetings with key business functions
- Create a one-page "Business + Compliance Charter" to define shared goals
- Review one existing process and reframe it through a win-win lens
- List of 3 business partners you can proactively support this month

Self-Assessment Tool

Statement	Never	Sometimes	Often	Always
I frame compliance advice in a way that supports business goals	☐	☐	☐	☐
I work with business teams early in their planning process	☐	☐	☐	☐
I suggest compliant alternatives, not just problems	☐	☐	☐	☐
I understand the commercial pressures and priorities	☐	☐	☐	☐

Tip: Score yourself to identify if your mindset leans toward control or collaboration. Always = 4. Never = 1

🚀 Next Habit: Start Listening Deeper

Compliance isn't just about interpreting rules—it's about understanding the **intent** behind them.

In **Habit 5**, we'll talk about how effective compliance professionals **listen deeply to regulators**—and use that understanding to guide their firms with confidence.

📖 *Next up: Habit 5 – Seek First to Understand (Regulatory Intent)*

⏸ Pause & Reflect: Are You Practicing What You've Learned?

Before we dive into the next habit, let's take a moment to pause.

You've just read through the first **four habits**—the foundation of an effective compliance mindset:

1. **Be Proactive**: Anticipate and prevent risks instead of reacting to them

2. **Begin with Compliance by Design**: Embed compliance from the start, not after the mess

3. **Put First Things First**: Prioritize the most critical obligations

4. **Think Win-Win**: Align compliance with business goals to enable growth

Now ask yourself—not just conceptually, but *honestly*—how well are you practicing these habits in your current role?

Take 10 minutes. Find a quiet corner. Reflect and jot down your thoughts:

1. Which of the four habits comes most naturally to me? Why?

2. Which habit do I struggle with the most? What's holding me back?

3. What was one "aha" moment I had while reading the past chapters?

4. What is *one* small action I can take tomorrow to move closer to becoming a more effective compliance leader?

📑 **Mini Quiz: Did You Get the Core Concepts?**

Q1. What is the key difference between reactive and proactive compliance?
A. Proactive compliance focuses on fixing issues once they're raised
B. Proactive compliance aims to identify and address risks before they materialize
C. Proactive compliance means strict policy enforcement
Answer: B

Q2. "Compliance by design" means:
A. Writing policies after a product is launched
B. Auditing once the business process is live
C. Embedding compliance early in the design and planning phase
Answer: C

Q3. A compliance prioritization matrix typically considers which two factors?
A. Popularity and budget
B. Legal language and reporting frequency
C. Risk impact and probability of occurrence
Answer: C

Q4. Thinking win-win means:
A. Finding a way for compliance and business to both succeed

B. Letting the business win to build relationships
C. Saying yes to all requests
Answer: A

Q5. If business teams see compliance as a blocker, what's the most productive approach?
A. Avoid interaction with them
B. Provide alternative, compliant solutions that support their goals
C. Enforce stricter review cycles
Answer: B

Q6. Which of the following tools helps align compliance with business goals?
A. The Compliance Penalty Tracker
B. Legal Dictionary
C. Compliance Playbooks and Business Charters
Answer: C

30-Second Gut Check

Without overthinking, answer YES or NO to the following:

- Do I feel seen and heard by business leaders in my organization?

- Have I ever prevented a crisis by raising a risk early?

- Do I know which compliance areas our regulator cares most about?

- Can I explain compliance risks in a way that resonates with commercial teams?

If you said "NO" to any of the above—great. You've just identified where your next growth opportunity lies.

Habit	Where I Stand	Next Step
Be Proactive	☑ Strong Medium Weak	☑ ☑ ________________________
Compliance by Design	☑ Strong Medium Weak	☑ ☑ ________________________
Prioritizing Critical Requirements	☑ Strong Medium Weak	☑ ☑ ________________________
Thinking Win-Win	☑ Strong Medium Weak	☑ ☑ ________________________

Habit 5: Seek First to Understand

"Don't just follow the rule. Understand the 'why' behind it."

🕵 The Story: A Policy That Backfired

Maya had just wrapped up the firm's new AML policy. It was textbook-perfect: aligned with regulatory clauses, full of technical terms, and had footnotes from FATF guidance.

Yet, during an inspection, the regulator pointed to a simple issue: the firm's internal thresholds for unusual activity reporting didn't align with *actual risk exposure*.

"You're compliant on paper," the regulator said. *"But you've missed the purpose of the rule: early detection and meaningful escalation."*

That comment shook Maya. She had been so focused on literal compliance, she'd overlooked the **regulatory intent**—to create a system that *works* in the real world, not just one that *reads well* in audits.

From that point on, Maya changed her approach. She started reading between the lines of guidance papers, attending regulator roundtables, reviewing enforcement decisions, and—most importantly—asking, *"What's the outcome the regulator truly wants here?"*

🎯 The Principle: Intent > Interpretation

Most compliance failures don't come from ignoring laws; they come from **misinterpreting their spirit**.

Understanding regulatory intent is about:

- Knowing *why* a rule exists

- Appreciating what problem, it seeks to prevent

- Aligning internal processes with the regulator's expectations—not just their words

Regulators care about outcomes:

- Are you protecting customers?

- Are you managing risk in substance, not just form?

- Are your controls living in practice, not just in policy folders?

When you seek to understand first, **you reduce friction, anticipate scrutiny, and build trust.**

🛠 Practical Strategies to Build This Habit

🔍 1. Read Enforcement Cases and Thematic Reviews

- Extract patterns: what principles do regulators keep coming back to?

- Ask: *What does this decision teach us about expectation vs. wording?*

■▌ 2. Follow Regulator Speeches and Newsletters

- These often contain more honest insight than formal rules

- Watch for "signal phrases": "firms are expected to…" or "a good practice is…"

🤝 3. Engage in Two-Way Dialogue

- Ask regulators clarifying questions when permitted

- Attend consultations and industry roundtables

📄 4. Include 'Regulatory Intent' Notes in Policies

- Add a small section explaining *why* the control exists—not just *what* it is

- Helps staff understand purpose, not just process

👨‍🏫 5. Train Teams on Regulatory Philosophy

- Create awareness: rules are the *minimum*, intent is the *benchmark*

- Use real stories of firms that "technically complied but still failed"

⚠️ Common Challenges—and How to Overcome Them

Challenge	Solution
Teams focus only on literal interpretation	Include intent notes and outcome-based training

Challenge	Solution
Fear of engaging directly with regulators	Engage through industry forums or clarify via legal counsel
Internal stakeholders want "black-and-white" rules	Share cases where ambiguity led to penalties
Confusion between global and local standards	Map obligations with context; explain jurisdictional nuances

Dialogue: Lena and Omar on a New Data Regulation

Lena (Compliance Consultant): "The new regulation mandates consent before data sharing. But what's the real concern here?"

Omar (Data Officer): "Probably customer privacy and informed control."

Lena: "Exactly. So, instead of just updating our checkbox wording, let's revamp the customer journey to make consent *meaningful.*

Omar: "That's next-level. Let's design an intuitive opt-in flow—and explain it in plain English."

Quick Tips

Ask: *What is the regulator trying to protect? Who are they trying to empower?*

- In internal reviews, frame feedback like a regulator would

- Create a "Regulator Radar" board—track trends in decisions and speeches

- Practice rewriting complex rules into plain-language objectives

Reflection Questions

1. Do I understand the *purpose* behind the rules I'm enforcing?

2. Have I reviewed any enforcement case studies recently?

3. Am I helping others see beyond black-letter law?

4. Do my policies reflect practical substance or theoretical compliance?

Action Steps

- Choose one recent regulation and write a "Why This Rule Exists" note for your team

- Conduct a team session analyzing 1–2 enforcement cases and extracting intent

- Add a new column to your compliance obligation tracker: *"Regulatory Purpose"*

- Revisit one internal policy and update it to reflect real-world risk alignment

Self-Assessment Tool

Statement	Never	Sometimes	Often	Always
I seek to understand the *why* behind every regulatory requirement	☐	☐	☐	☐
I read regulator speeches, reviews, or enforcement cases regularly	☐	☐	☐	☐
I help others interpret rules with practical, outcome-based thinking	☐	☐	☐	☐
I align internal controls with regulator expectations—not just texts	☐	☐	☐	☐
I embed regulatory intent into training and internal policies	☐	☐	☐	☐

Tip: If you scored low here, start with just one new habit: read one enforcement case each week and ask, *"What principle is being reinforced?"*

Habit 6: Synergize

Collaborate Cross-Functionally

📝 The Story: Silos, Turf Wars, and a Missed Opportunity

The audit report was scathing. A client's high-risk transaction had slipped through the cracks because no one team had full visibility. Compliance flagged the client in the onboarding stage, but Operations thought it was cleared. Legal had their doubts, but assumed the risk team had done a full review. Everyone was working hard—just not together.

During the post-mortem, it became clear: the problem wasn't lack of controls. It was **lack of collaboration**.

Ravi, the MLRO, sighed. *"If someone had just picked up the phone and connected the dots, this could've been prevented."*

This wasn't a failure of intelligence. It was a failure of integration.

🌐 The Principle: Compliance Is a Team Sport

Compliance doesn't live in one department. It breathes through:

- Ops teams flagging anomalies

- Sales understanding onboarding red flags

- Tech embedding system controls

- HR identifying misconduct risks

- Finance tracking suspicious transactions

- And yes, Compliance—pulling it all together

Effective compliance professionals don't just *coordinate* across departments—they **collaborate**, co-create, and build bridges.

That's synergy.

🛠 Practical Strategies to Build This Habit

⚙ 1. Map Your Stakeholders

- Create a cross-functional matrix: who owns what compliance touchpoint?

- Identify communication gaps and duplication risks

🗓 2. Run Monthly Compliance Roundtables

- Invite Legal, Risk, IT, Ops, Sales, HR

- Make it informal and conversational

- Use real scenarios, not just reports

📝 3. Create Shared Compliance Playbooks

- Co-author SOPs for client onboarding, transaction monitoring, investigations

- Use visual workflows showing team dependencies

🤝 4. Set Up Compliance Liaisons

- Assign a "compliance buddy" or champion in each department

- Train them to be the first line of compliance voice

💬 5. Use Collaboration Tools Wisely

- Shared dashboards, Slack/Teams channels, compliance alerts

- Make collaboration visible, not just verbal

⚠️ Common Challenges—and How to Overcome Them

Challenge	Solution
Silo mentality: "That's not our job"	Show how shared risk leads to shared consequences
Compliance is left out of key decisions	Proactively ask to be included in planning phases
Miscommunication and role confusion	Use RACI charts (Responsible, Accountable, Consulted, Informed)
Different departments speak different "languages"	Translate compliance risks into each department's context

💬 Dialogue: Aisha Bridges Compliance and Tech

49 | Ten Habits of effective Compliance Professionals

Aisha (Compliance Lead): "This new trading app needs real-time AML checks. Can tech help?"

Imran (Tech Head): "If you'd told me last month, yes. We're already locked into the current build."

Aisha: "Let's meet weekly during your sprint planning. I'll embed controls as you develop."

Imran: *(smiling)* "That's the first time someone from Compliance offered to work at our pace."

Quick Tips (Sidebar)

- Use whiteboards and diagrams to explain processes in team workshops

- Rotate compliance team members into other department meetings

- Send short compliance updates tailored to each function

- Start your meetings with *"What's one issue we're not seeing?"* to encourage candor

Reflection Questions

1. Do I understand how other departments perceive compliance?

2. Have I ever built a compliance process *with* another department, not just *for* them?

3. Do I have go-to contacts in each key function?

4. What tools could improve transparency and coordination right now?

Action Steps

- Create a cross-functional compliance map: people, processes, and points of overlap

- Identify one department where collaboration is weak—and initiate a dialogue

- Host a "Compliance Collaboration Day" where teams present joint risk cases

- Pick a recurring process (e.g. client onboarding) and invite feedback from all departments involved

---

Self-Assessment Tool

Statement	Never	Sometimes	Often	Always
I collaborate with other departments regularly on compliance	☐	☐	☐	☐
I understand how my work intersects Ops, Legal, Risk, etc.	☐	☐	☐	☐
I involve others in creating compliance SOPs and controls	☐	☐	☐	☐
I use tools or workflows that encourage transparency	☐	☐	☐	☐
I have compliance liaisons/champions in non-compliance teams	☐	☐	☐	☐

Tip: If "Never" or "Sometimes" dominates your answers, it's time to expand your circle

Continuous Professional Development

▧ The Story: The Compliance Officer Who Got Left Behind

Rohit had been in the compliance world for over a decade. He was sharp, experienced, and confident. But during a recent internal meeting about implementing a new RegTech tool, he found himself lost.

Words like "natural language processing," "machine learning," and "integrated analytics" flew around the room. Everyone seemed to understand—except him.

When the younger compliance analyst, Anjali, started mapping risk indicators using data visualization dashboards, Rohit realized something unsettling: **he wasn't obsolete, but he was dangerously close.**

Later that day, he typed into Google: *"Courses to understand AI in compliance."*

That was the moment he made a critical decision—not to catch up, but to stay ahead.

🎯 The Principle: If You're Not Learning, You're Falling Behind

Compliance is no longer static. Regulations change. Risks evolve. Technology redefines how we work.

The most effective compliance professionals treat **continuous learning** not as an optional extra—but as a **core responsibility**.

Sharpening the saw means:

- Keeping your legal and regulatory knowledge current

- Gaining technical literacy (data, systems, analytics, AI)

- Developing soft skills, communication, negotiation, leadership

- Learning from mistakes, peers, and industry at large

In short: the sharper your mind, the stronger your impact.

🛠️ Practical Strategies to Build This Habit

📇 1. Create a Personal Learning Plan

- Identify gaps in your legal, technical, and soft skills

- Allocate time monthly for learning—like you would for meetings

🖥️ 2. Leverage Online Learning Platforms

- Coursera, edX, Udemy for technical or global content

- ACAMS, ICA, IAPP, and local regulators for certifications and updates

📰 3. Subscribe to the Right Knowledge Sources

- Regulatory authority newsletters (DFSA, FSRA, FATF, etc.)

- Industry blogs, compliance podcasts, LinkedIn thought leaders

🤝 4. Join Professional Communities

- Participate in webinars, conferences, or forums

- Join or start a compliance peer learning group in your city or firm

🗣 5. Teach to Learn

- Host lunch-and-learn sessions

- Mentor junior staff—you'll reinforce your own expertise while helping others

⚠ Common Challenges—and How to Overcome Them

Challenge	Solution
"No time to learn"	Schedule it like a meeting. 30 mins per week is a strong start
Learning feels overwhelming	Break it down: 1 skill/month or 1 article/week
No access to learning budget	Use free content or request access as part of performance goals
Unsure what to learn next	Ask your boss, peers, or follow trends, what skills are in demand?

💬 Dialogue: Lena Encourages Rohit to Upskill

Rohit: "Honestly, I've never worked with analytics dashboards before. This new AML software feels intimidating."

Lena: "That's okay. You've got the experience. Let's pair up—you take the data course; I'll Walk you through the dashboard."

Rohit: "Feels strange being the learner again."

Lena: "Stranger would be pretending you don't need to learn."

💡 Quick Tips (Sidebar)

- Block "Learning Hour" every Friday on your calendar

- Read one enforcement action a week and extract the lesson

- Follow 3 compliance thought leaders on LinkedIn or Substack

- Build personal knowledge bank—summarize everything you learn

Reflection Questions

1. What skill or tool have I avoided because it feels outside my comfort zone?

2. When was the last time I attended a compliance-related workshop or webinar?

3. How often do I update my compliance knowledge intentionally—not reactively?

4. Do I have a learning goal this quarter or this year?

✅ Action Steps

- Write a 3-month learning roadmap with one focus area per month

- Identify one soft skill (e.g. influencing) and one technical skill (e.g. Excel modeling, data analysis) to improve

- Join an online compliance community or LinkedIn group

- Host a "Learning Roundtable" where your team shares new insights

Self-Assessment Tool

Statement	Never	Sometimes	Often	Always
I intentionally allocate time to learn new compliance knowledge	☐	☐	☐	☐
I stay updated on regulatory trends and changes	☐	☐	☐	☐
I seek to improve both technical and communication skills	☐	☐	☐	☐
I use online platforms or courses for continuous development	☐	☐	☐	☐
I share what I learn with others to deepen understanding	☐	☐	☐	☐

Tip: Even 15 minutes a day = over 90 hours a year. Small habits. Big impact.

Next Up: Monitoring with Insight, Not Just Oversight

Now that your skills are growing, it's time to apply them.

In **Habit 8**, we'll explore how to move from manual checks to intelligent monitoring using data—so your compliance program becomes a predictive powerhouse.

Habit 8: Use Data as Your Compass

Data-Driven Compliance Monitoring

✳ **The Story: The Report That Changed Everything**

Anita, the Head of Compliance at a regional bank, had spent months preparing for the board meeting. But this time, she did something different.

Instead of walking in with a slide deck full of policies, audit timelines, and upcoming regulatory changes, she walked in with a **dashboard.**

It showed trends in transaction monitoring exceptions, flagged jurisdictions, overdue customer reviews, and training completion rates—broken down by the business unit.

No jargon. Just insight.

The CFO leaned forward.

"Wait, why is the East Region showing a 42% spike in alerts last month?"

That single chart sparked a 45-minute strategy conversation.

For the first time, **compliance had the room's full attention**—not as a gatekeeper, but as a risk-informed decision-maker.

🔍 The Principle: What Gets Measured, Gets Managed

Compliance today cannot run on gut feeling and scattered spreadsheets.

To be truly effective, compliance must become **data-literate** and **data-led**—translating monitoring into meaning, and checks into insights.

Data-driven compliance means:

- Tracking the *right* metrics, not just what's easy to collect

- Identifying risk patterns early—not after the audit report

- Creating visibility across the organization

- Moving from reactive reports to predictive indicators

In short, **data is your compass**, guiding where to act, what to fix, and how to improve.

🛠️ Practical Strategies to Build This Habit

📈 1. Define Compliance KPIs and KRIs

- Examples: STR turnaround time, overdue reviews, exceptions closed, employee training scores

- Segment by region, department, product line

📊 2. Build a Risk Monitoring Dashboard

- Start with Excel, Power BI, or Google Data Studio

- Track trends over time—not just snapshots

3. Automate Where Possible

- Use workflow tools or RegTech solutions to flag anomalies in real-time

- Integrate systems: KYC, CRM, trade surveillance, HR

4. Report Visually and Clearly

- Use heatmaps, bar charts, trend lines

- Tailor dashboards for different stakeholders (Ops vs. Board vs. Audit)

5. Use Data to Drive Conversations

- Don't just submit reports—interpret them

- Recommend actions based on insights: *"This spike means we should…"*

⚠ Common Challenges—and How to Overcome Them

Challenge	Solution
Too much data, not enough insight	Focus on 5–10 core metrics tied to risk and regulatory outcomes
Compliance lacks access to core systems	Build alliances with IT and data owners
Data is messy or inconsistent	Start small; define a "single source of truth"
Resistance to dashboards	Show how insights support business objectives, not just audits

Dialogue: Anjali & Ravi Explore Monitoring Evolution

59 | Ten Habits of effective Compliance Professionals

Anjali (Junior Compliance Analyst): "We've been reviewing STRs manually. Takes forever."

Ravi (MLRO): "Manual reviews have limits. Let's see if we can set filters or thresholds in our monitoring tool."

Anjali: "You mean use logic to surface only high-risk cases?"

Ravi: "Exactly. That way we focus energy where it matters—and we can show the board measurable risk reduction."

💡 **Quick Tips (Sidebar)**

- Build a "Compliance Metric of the Month" campaign internally

- Create a red-amber-green dashboard to show control health

60 | Ten Habits of effective Compliance Professionals

- Tie data insights to business impact: "X% drop in STR backlog = lower regulatory risk"

- Track training effectiveness through quiz scores and completion delays

Reflection Questions

1. What compliance metrics am I currently tracking—and why?

2. Do I review trends over time, or only react to incidents?

3. Am I using visuals to communicate compliance risks to leadership?

4. Could automation free up time for deeper compliance work?

Action Steps

- Define your top 5 compliance KPIs and track them weekly

- Build a basic dashboard using Excel or Google Sheets

- Review your last compliance report, can you turn it into a visual story?

- Ask IT or analytics teams for support in integrating compliance data flows

Self-Assessment Tool

Statement	Never	Sometimes	Often	Always
I use data to monitor compliance activities and risks	☐	☐	☐	☐
I present compliance insights visually to stakeholders	☐	☐	☐	☐

Statement	Never	Sometimes	Often	Always
I track trends in key compliance areas over time	☐	☐	☐	☐
I use compliance dashboards or tools to prioritize risks	☐	☐	☐	☐
I collaborate with IT/data teams to improve compliance intelligence	☐	☐	☐	☐

Tip: Even a simple dashboard with 3 KPIs is a powerful start. Progress > Perfection.

Habit 9: Build Culture

Integrity Over Enforcement

🗣 The Story: The Whistle That Was Never Blown

At GlobalTrade Corp, a junior employee named Fahad stumbled upon something odd—a consistent pattern of over-invoicing with one of the firm's largest vendors. He felt uncomfortable. But there was no clear place to report it confidentially. The ethics hotline was barely mentioned. And when he asked a colleague what to do, he was warned: *"Just stay quiet—people who raise issues here don't last long."*

So, Fahad stayed quiet.

Three months later, the issue exploded—picked up by an investigative journalist. By then, it was too late. The firm's reputation took a major hit. Regulators launched a full investigation. Internally, the compliance officer was devastated.

"If we had built a culture where people felt safe to speak, this would've never gone public."

The firm had compliance policies. But not a **compliance culture.**

⚙️ The Principle: Culture Is the Ultimate Control

Rules can be bypassed. Systems can fail. But culture? That's what people follow when no one's watching.

Compliance culture is the set of shared values, beliefs, and behaviors that define how seriously people take ethics, integrity, and accountability—even when enforcement isn't watching.

It's what turns:

- "Mandatory training" into *meaningful awareness*

- "Tick-box policies" into *real-world practices*

- "Fear of punishment" into *personal ownership*

Great compliance professionals don't just monitor—they **shape mindsets** and **model integrity.**

🔧 Practical Strategies to Build This Habit

🗣️ 1. Promote Speak-Up Culture

- Regularly remind staff about whistleblowing channels

- Protect confidentiality and ensure zero retaliation

- Recognize those who raise concerns—even if the outcome is neutral

2. Humanize Training

- Use case studies, storytelling, and real-world consequences

- Tailor sessions by department—make it personal and relevant

- Include leadership in delivering training, not just ticking a box

3. Get Leadership Buy-In

- Ask senior executives to publicly share their values on ethics

- Include compliance KPIs in leadership scorecards

- Encourage "tone at the top" to become "echo from the middle"

4. Measure Culture

- Use anonymous culture surveys with questions like: *"Do you feel safe raising concerns?"* or *"Do people in your team take shortcuts?"*

- Track ethical decision-making confidence over time

5. Embed Ethics in Everyday Conversations

- Start meetings with short "integrity moments"

- Highlight small stories of ethical behavior—not just big headlines

- Encourage managers to ask: *"What's the right thing to do here?"*

Common Challenges—and How to Overcome Them

Challenge	Solution
Fear of retaliation from speaking up	Build strong whistleblower protection policies and communications

Challenge	Solution
Leadership pays lip service to ethics	Tie culture goals to executive KPIs and public messaging
Training is boring and forgettable	Make it interactive, scenario-based, and department-specific
Compliance seen as "policing"	Shift to coaching and storytelling roles—model the culture yourself

💬 **Dialogue: Aisha Talks Culture with HR**

Aisha (Head of Compliance): "I need your help. Our speak-up culture isn't working."

Neha (Head of HR): "We run training every year…"

Aisha: "Yes, but it's not enough. People don't feel safe. We need managers to encourage openness in team meetings."

Neha: "So not just policies—but habits."

Aisha: "Exactly. Let's start a monthly ethics story campaign. Positive reinforcement."

💡 **Quick Tips**

- Use employee onboarding to set tone: "Here, we do the right thing—even when it's hard."

- Make compliance training a dialogue, not a download

- Celebrate ethical decisions—even small ones

- Display visual cues: posters, reminders, stories of integrity on notice boards or intranet

❄️ **Reflection Questions**

1. If I asked five employees, would they know how to report unethical conduct?

2. Do people feel psychologically safe to admit mistakes or raise concerns?

3. Are compliance conversations proactive or only incident-driven?

4. What story does leadership behavior tell about our compliance culture?

✅ Action Steps

- Launch a 2-question monthly "Ethics Pulse" survey to track sentiment

- Organize a cross-functional ethics panel to share real dilemmas and decisions

- Propose culture KPIs for leadership: training participation, issue reporting, etc.

- Create a repository of mini case studies on ethical dilemmas (true or anonymized)

Self-Assessment Tool

Statement	Never	Sometimes	Often	Always
Employees feel safe reporting compliance concerns	☐	☐	☐	☐
Compliance is positioned as a shared responsibility, not a watchdog	☐	☐	☐	☐
Leadership models ethical behavior consistently	☐	☐	☐	☐
We measure culture through surveys or pulse checks	☐	☐	☐	☐
We share stories that celebrate integrity and good decisions	☐	☐	☐	☐

Tip: Even one strong voice can start a culture shift. Be that voice.

Habit 10: Lead Ethically

Beyond Compliance

The Story: The MLRO Who Resigned on Principle

Zara was the Money Laundering Reporting Officer (MLRO) at a well-known investment firm. Her job was difficult, but she took pride in doing it with integrity.

Then came the deal.

A politically connected client wanted to invest through a complex offshore structure. The onboarding paperwork was clean—but Zara's gut and experience raised red flags. She flagged the risks, documented her concerns, and asked for enhanced due diligence.

The CEO disagreed. *"Let it go. We can't afford to lose this client."*

Zara stood her ground. She pushed back with reports, recommendations, and regulatory references. Eventually, she escalated the matter to the Board.

When it was clear that the firm would proceed regardless, she did something radical: **she resigned.**

Six months later, that client was linked to a major corruption scandal. The firm's reputation crumbled.

Zara's quiet strength became legendary in the industry. Not because she was right—but because she **chose ethics over convenience**, values over employment, leadership over compromise.

The Principle: When Compliance Ends, Ethics Begins

Compliance sets the minimum. **Ethics sets the direction.**

Great compliance professionals don't stop at ticking boxes. They lead. They influence. They uphold what's right, especially when it's inconvenient.

Ethical leadership means:

- Speaking truth to power—even when it's uncomfortable

- Taking accountability, not hiding behind policies

- Setting an example for others, not just issuing instructions

- Asking not just *"Is this legal?"* but *"Is this right?"*

In a complex world, ethical leadership becomes your compass—especially when the rules are unclear or evolving.

🛠️ Practical Strategies to Build This Habit

⚙️ 1. Develop Your Ethical Decision Framework

- Ask: *Is this legal? Is it fair? Would I defend this in public?*
- Document gray-area decisions with rationale and escalation steps

🎙️ 2. Model Transparency

- Share your dilemmas (where appropriate) to foster openness
- Acknowledge mistakes and explain how you handled them

🗣️ 3. Influence Without Authority

- Use storytelling and logic to build trust with senior stakeholders
- Build informal coalitions to support ethical stances

🛡️ 4. Know Your Red Lines

- Define your personal and professional limits
- Prepare your strategy in case you're asked to cross them

🧩 5. Mentor and Multiply

- Help junior professionals develop their ethical muscle
- Create a values-based leadership culture in your team

⚠️ Common Challenges—and How to Overcome Them

Challenge	Solution
Pressure from senior leadership to ignore red flags	Use documented escalation, external benchmarking, legal review

Challenge	Solution
Fear of retaliation or isolation	Build networks, document everything, protect your position
Ethics seen as "optional" when under pressure	Share case studies where ethical lapses caused real damage
Difficulty saying "no" to powerful stakeholders	Say *"I understand the pressure, but here's what's at stake"*

Dialogue: Omar Encourages Lena to Take a Stand

Lena (Compliance Officer): "The deal doesn't feel right, but everyone's on board."

Omar (Ex-regulator turned advisor): "Then this is your moment. Your role isn't to follow the crowd—it's to be the conscience of the firm."

Lena: "I could lose my seat at the table."

Omar: "Or you could gain something more powerful—respect, and self-trust."

Quick Tips Keep a journal of ethical crossroads you encounter—reflect on them

- Build relationships with independent board members or audit committees

- Roleplay difficult conversations before you have them

- Always have a "Plan B"—you can't lead ethically if you're cornered without options

Reflection Questions

1. What are my non-negotiable values as a professional?

2. Have I ever stayed silent when I should have spoken up? Why?

3. Who inspires me as an ethical leader—and why?

4. Do I mentor others in making value-based decisions?

✅ Action Steps

- Create your personal "Ethics Checklist" for gray-zone decisions

- Review your last big decision, did it align with your values?

- Speak to a trusted mentor about an ethical challenge you're facing

- Initiate a value-based conversation with your team this week

📊 Self-Assessment Tool

Statement	Never	Sometimes	Often	Always
I consider ethical implications, not just legal requirements	☐	☐	☐	☐
I am willing to speak up even if it's unpopular or risky	☐	☐	☐	☐
I model integrity in difficult or high-pressure situations	☐	☐	☐	☐
I help others build ethical judgment and courage	☐	☐	☐	☐
I have a clear set of personal red lines and values	☐	☐	☐	☐

Tip: Leadership begins when you stop asking for permission to do the right thing.

⏸ Pause & Reflect: Deepening the Final Five Habits

You've just explored the final five habits that elevate compliance professionals from technical experts to strategic leaders:

5. **Seek First to Understand** (Regulatory Intent)

6. **Synergize** (Collaborate Cross-Functionally)

7. **Sharpen the Saw** (Continuous Professional Development)

8. **Use Data as Your Compass** (Data-Driven Monitoring)

9. **Build Culture** (Integrity Over Enforcement)

10. **Lead Ethically** (Beyond Compliance)

These habits aren't about rules, they're about mindset, influence, and long-term value. Before we move to the conclusion, let's pause and lock in what you've learned.

Reflective Journal

Take a few minutes to jot down your answers. No overthinking, just honest reflection:

1. Which of the final five habits challenged me the most? Why?

2. Where have I seen poor collaboration or ethical gaps impact compliance?

3. What is one small change I can make to bring more integrity into my daily work?

4. How am I currently using data? How can I use it more meaningfully?

5. What's my long-term learning goal as a compliance professional?

📝 Quick Quiz: Check Your Understanding

Q1. Regulatory intent refers to: A. The exact legal language in a rule B. The underlying purpose or principle the rule aims to uphold C. How your firm interprets the rule internally
Answer: ✅ B

Q2. Cross-functional collaboration is most effective when: A. Compliance gives instructions to each team separately B. Everyone operates independently within their domain C. Teams co-create solutions with shared accountability
Answer: ✅ C

Q3. Continuous professional development involves: A. Annual AML training only
B. Ongoing learning across legal, technical, and interpersonal skills
C. Memorizing regulations
Answer: ✅ B

Q4. A key advantage of data-driven monitoring is A. Replacing policies entirely
B. Reducing compliance headcount
C. Identifying risks early and showing measurable insights
Answer: ✅ C

Q5. Ethical leadership means: A. Following the letter of the law strictly
B. Doing what's right, even when it's unpopular or risky

C. Avoiding decisions outside your policy manual

Answer: ☑ B

⌒ Gut Check: Quick Yes/No

- Have I ever chosen to stay silent when I should've spoken up?

- Do I regularly help others understand the "why" behind our policies?

- Am I known as a collaborative partner across functions?

- Have I invested in learning something new in the last 30 days?

- Can I explain our top compliance risks using data or visualizations?

Every "No" here is a learning opportunity, not a failure. Growth starts with awareness.

☑ Summary Self-Assessment Table

Habit	Where I Stand	Next Step
Understanding Regulatory Intent	☑ Strong Medium Weak	☑ ☑ _______________________
Cross-Functional Collaboration	☑ Strong Medium Weak	☑ ☑ _______________________
Continuous Learning	☑ Strong Medium Weak	☑ ☑ _______________________

Data-Driven Monitoring	☑ Strong Medium Weak	☑ ☑ ________________________
Building Integrity Culture	☑ Strong Medium Weak	☑ ☑ ________________________
Ethical Leadership	☑ Strong Medium Weak	☑ ☑ ________________________

▦ Conclusion: The Compliance Effectiveness Framework

You've journeyed through ten habits that define truly effective compliance professionals. But this isn't just a checklist. It's a **framework**. A way of thinking, leading, and enabling organizations to do the right thing, the smart way.

Let's bring everything together.

⚖ The 10 Habits Recap

Habit No.	Habit Title	Core Outcome
1	Be Proactive	Prevent risks before they become crises
2	Begin with Compliance by Design	Embed compliance early in all processes
3	Put First Things First	Focus on critical, high-impact priorities
4	Think Win-Win	Align compliance with business success

5	Seek First to Understand (Regulatory Intent)	Interpret and apply rules with insight
6	Synergize (Collaborate Cross-Functionally)	Break silos, build shared accountability
7	Sharpen the Saw (Continuous Learning)	Stay ahead through professional growth
8	Use Data as Your Compass	Monitor risk through intelligent metrics
9	Build Culture (Integrity Over Enforcement)	Foster behavior-driven compliance
10	Lead Ethically (Beyond Compliance)	Be the voice of principle and trust

The Compliance Effectiveness Pyramid

You can visualize these habits as a layered pyramid:

Level 1: Foundation – Personal Responsibility

- Habit 1: Be Proactive

- Habit 2: Compliance by Design

- Habit 3: Prioritize Critically

Level 2: Integration – Business Enablement

- Habit 4: Win-Win Thinking

- Habit 5: Understanding Regulatory Intent

- Habit 6: Cross-Functional Collaboration

Level 3: Maturity – Strategic Leadership

- Habit 7: Continuous Learning

- Habit 8: Data-Driven Monitoring

- Habit 9: Integrity Culture

- Habit 10: Ethical Leadership

Where to Go from Here

1. **Reflect on your current maturity level.** Which layer are you strong in? Which needs work?

2. **Create your 90-day Compliance Growth Plan.** Pick 2 habits to actively develop with goals and actions.

3. **Share this framework with your team.** Use it to spark conversations, build alignment, and raise standards.

4. **Revisit this book regularly.** New situations will reveal new layers of each habit.

🤝 Final Words: The Role Only You Can Play

Compliance isn't about stopping things. It's about enabling the right things to happen, the right way. In a world filled with change, risk, and noise, compliance professionals are becoming some of the most important navigators inside organizations.

Your credibility doesn't come from saying "no." It comes from asking better questions, giving smarter answers, and helping others do the right thing with confidence.

When you live these ten habits, you don't just do compliance. **You embody trust.**

Thank you for committing to this journey. The future of compliance is not only in systems or regulations. It's in people like you.

Let's build that future—habit by habit.

🔲 Optional: Self-Rating Summary Table (All Habits)

Habit	My Current Rating (1–5)	My Target (in 90 days)
Be Proactive		
Compliance by Design		
Prioritize Critically		
Win-Win Thinking		
Understanding Regulatory Intent		
Cross-Functional Collaboration		
Continuous Learning		
Data-Driven Monitoring		
Integrity Culture		
Ethical Leadership		

PART B- Case study scenarios based on 10 habits

Case Study: Navigating Compliance Challenges at Zenith Bank

Institution: Zenith Bank
Location: Metropolis City
Industry: Financial Services

Background

Zenith Bank, a mid-sized financial institution in Metropolis City, has built a reputation for innovation and customer-centric services. Recently, the bank has been preparing to launch a new digital payment platform aimed at enhancing customer convenience and expanding its market share. However, during the final stages of development, the compliance team, led by Chief Compliance Officer (CCO) Priya Desai, identified potential regulatory concerns related to data privacy and anti-money laundering (AML) compliance.

Problem Statement

The compliance team discovered that the new digital payment platform's data collection processes might not fully align with the latest data protection regulations. Additionally, the platform's transaction monitoring system was found to be inadequate for detecting suspicious activities, posing a risk of non-compliance with AML regulations. These issues could lead to regulatory penalties, reputational damage, and erosion of customer trust if not addressed promptly.

Application of 10 Habits

1. **Be Proactive: Anticipating Compliance Risks**

Action: Priya initiated a comprehensive risk assessment during the development phase of the digital platform, identifying potential compliance issues before the launch.

Outcome: Early detection allowed the team to address vulnerabilities proactively, preventing future regulatory breaches.

2. **Begin with Compliance by Design: Integrating Compliance into Development**

Action: The compliance team collaborated with the IT and product development teams to embed compliance requirements into the platform's architecture from the outset.

Outcome: This integration ensured that data privacy and AML controls were foundational elements of the platform, reducing the need for costly modifications later.

3. **Put First Things First: Prioritizing Critical Compliance Issues**

Action: Recognizing the severity of data privacy and AML risks, Priya prioritized these issues over less critical concerns, allocating resources and attention accordingly.

Outcome: Focused efforts led to the swift resolution of the most pressing compliance challenges, aligning the project with regulatory expectations.

4. **Think Win-Win: Aligning Compliance with Business Objectives**

Action: Priya worked with business leaders to demonstrate how robust compliance measures could enhance customer trust and provide a competitive edge.

Outcome: This alignment fostered a collaborative approach, ensuring that compliance was seen as a business enabler rather than a hindrance.

5. Seek First to Understand: Grasping Regulatory Intent

Action: The compliance team engaged with legal experts and regulatory bodies to fully understand the intent behind data protection and AML regulations.

Outcome: A deeper understanding allowed the team to implement controls that met both the letter and spirit of the law.

6. Synergize: Collaborating Across Functions

Action: Regular cross-functional meetings were established, bringing together compliance, IT, legal, and business development teams to address compliance challenges collectively.

Outcome: This collaboration led to innovative solutions that balanced regulatory requirements with business goals.

7. Sharpen the Saw: Continuous Learning and Adaptation

Action: Priya encouraged her team to pursue ongoing education on emerging compliance trends and regulatory changes, particularly in the fintech space.

Outcome: The team's enhanced knowledge kept Zenith Bank ahead of compliance developments, reducing the risk of future issues.

8. Use Data as Your Compass: Data-Driven Compliance Monitoring

Action: Advanced analytics were employed to monitor transaction data in real-time, identifying patterns indicative of potential AML violations.

Outcome: Data-driven insights improved the effectiveness of compliance monitoring, enabling prompt responses to suspicious activities.

9. **Build Culture: Fostering Integrity Over Enforcement**

Action: A culture of compliance was cultivated through training programs and leadership messages emphasizing ethical behavior and personal accountability.

Outcome: Employees internalized compliance values, leading to self-regulation and a reduced need for enforcement actions.

10. **Lead Ethically: Exemplifying Integrity Beyond Compliance**

Action: Priya led by example, making transparent decisions and standing firm on compliance matters, even when facing pressure to expedite the platform's launch.

Outcome: Her ethical leadership reinforced the importance of compliance throughout the organization, setting a standard for others to follow.

Outcome

By applying these ten habits, Zenith Bank successfully addressed the compliance challenges associated with its new digital payment platform. The proactive and integrated approach not only ensured regulatory compliance but also enhanced the platform's security and customer trust. The collaborative efforts across departments led to innovative solutions that balanced business objectives with compliance requirements. Furthermore, fostering a culture of integrity and continuous learning positioned Zenith Bank to navigate future compliance challenges effectively.

Case Study: Upholding Compliance and Integrity at Prestige Private Bank

Institution: Prestige Private Bank

Location: Global Financial Hub

Industry: Private Banking and Wealth Management

Background

Prestige Private Bank, renowned for its bespoke financial services to high-net-worth individuals (HNWIs), has built a reputation for discretion and excellence. The bank offers a range of services, including wealth management, estate planning, and investment advisory. Given the complex nature of its clientele's financial activities, the bank faces heightened scrutiny from regulators, necessitating robust compliance frameworks.

Problem Statement

During a routine internal audit, the compliance team, led by Chief Compliance Officer (CCO) **Jonathan Reed**, identified several accounts with transaction patterns indicative of potential money laundering activities. These accounts belonged to politically exposed persons (PEPs) and clients from jurisdictions known for high financial crime risks. The transactions involved large, rapid movements of funds through multiple offshore entities, raising red flags for regulatory compliance.

The bank faced the challenge of addressing these potential compliance breaches without compromising client relationships or its reputation. Failure to act could result in severe regulatory penalties, legal ramifications, and damage to the bank's standing in the financial community.

Application of 10 Habits

1. **Be Proactive: Anticipating Compliance Risks**

Action: Jonathan initiated an immediate, comprehensive review of all high-risk client accounts, focusing on transaction patterns and the effectiveness of existing monitoring systems.

Outcome: This proactive approach allowed the bank to identify and assess potential compliance issues before they escalated into regulatory violations.

2. **Begin with Compliance by Design: Integrating Compliance into Client Onboarding**

Action: The compliance team collaborated with the client relations department to embed stringent compliance checks into the client onboarding process, particularly for PEPs and clients from high-risk jurisdictions.

Outcome: Enhanced due diligence procedures ensured that compliance considerations were integral to client acceptance, reducing the risk of onboarding clients with potential compliance issues.

3. Put First Things First: Prioritizing Critical Compliance Issues

Action: Recognizing the severity of the potential money laundering activities, Jonathan prioritized the investigation of these accounts over other compliance matters, allocating necessary resources and attention.

Outcome: Focused efforts led to a thorough understanding of the issues at hand, facilitating timely and effective remediation.

4. Think Win-Win: Aligning Compliance with Client Relationships

Action: Jonathan engaged with relationship managers to discuss the importance of compliance in maintaining the bank's integrity and client trust, emphasizing that robust compliance measures protect both the bank and its clients.

Outcome: This alignment fostered a collaborative approach, ensuring that compliance efforts were seen as enhancing, rather than hindering, client relationships.

5. Seek First to Understand: Grasping Regulatory Intent

Action: The compliance team consulted with legal experts and regulatory bodies to fully understand the intent behind anti-money laundering (AML) regulations and how they applied to private banking operations.

Outcome: A deeper understanding enabled the team to implement controls that met both the letter and spirit of the law, ensuring comprehensive compliance.

6. Synergize: Collaborating Across Functions

Action: Regular cross-functional meetings were established, bringing together compliance, legal, client relations, and operations teams to address the identified compliance challenges collectively.

Outcome: This collaboration led to the development of holistic solutions that balanced regulatory requirements with client service excellence.

7. Sharpen the Saw: Continuous Learning and Adaptation

Action: Jonathan encouraged his team to pursue ongoing education on emerging compliance trends, particularly in the realm of AML and PEP risk management.

Outcome: The team's enhanced knowledge kept Prestige Private Bank ahead of regulatory developments, reducing the risk of future compliance issues.

8. Use Data as Your Compass: Data-Driven Compliance Monitoring

Action: Advanced analytics and machine learning tools were employed to enhance transaction monitoring systems, enabling real-time detection of suspicious activities.

Outcome: Data-driven insights improved the effectiveness of compliance monitoring, allowing for prompt identification and investigation of potential money laundering activities.

9. Build Culture: Fostering Integrity Over Enforcement

Action: A culture of compliance was cultivated through regular training programs and leadership messages emphasizing ethical behavior and personal accountability.

Outcome: Employees internalized compliance values, leading to self-regulation and a reduced need for enforcement actions.

10. Lead Ethically: Exemplifying Integrity Beyond Compliance

Action: Jonathan led by example, making transparent decisions and standing firm on compliance matters, even when facing pressure from influential clients and internal stakeholders.

Outcome: His ethical leadership reinforced the importance of compliance throughout the organization, setting a standard for others to follow.

Outcome

By applying these ten habits, Prestige Private Bank successfully addressed the compliance challenges associated with its high-risk client accounts. The proactive and integrated approach not only ensured regulatory compliance but also enhanced the bank's reputation for integrity and diligence. The collaborative efforts across departments led to innovative solutions that balanced client service with stringent compliance requirements. Furthermore, fostering a culture of integrity and continuous learning positioned Prestige Private Bank to navigate future compliance challenges effectively.

Case Study: Compliance Failures at Global Trust Bank

Institution: Global Trust Bank
Location: International Financial Center
Industry: Banking and Financial Services

Background

Global Trust Bank was a prominent player in the international banking sector, offering a wide range of services including retail banking, wealth management, and investment banking. Despite its esteemed position, the bank encountered severe regulatory penalties due to multiple compliance breaches that spanned several years.

Compliance Failures and Consequences

1. **Failure to Prevent Money Laundering Activities**

Issue: The bank's inadequate anti-money laundering (AML) controls allowed illicit funds to be processed without detection.

Consequence: Regulatory authorities imposed a fine of $500 million for violations of AML regulations.

2. Unauthorized Creation of Customer Accounts

Issue: Employees, under pressure to meet unrealistic sales targets, opened unauthorized accounts without customer consent.

Consequence: The bank faced a $250 million penalty and suffered significant reputational damage.

3. Inadequate Data Protection Measures

Issue: Weak cybersecurity protocols led to a data breach compromising sensitive customer information.

Consequence: A $300 million fine was levied, and the bank was mandated to overhaul its data security infrastructure.

4. Non-Compliance with Sanctions Regulations

Issue: The bank facilitated transactions with entities in sanctioned countries, violating international sanctions laws.

Consequence: A $400 million penalty was imposed, and certain international operations were suspended.

5. Misrepresentation of Financial Products

Issue: The bank misled clients about the risks associated with certain investment products.

Consequence: Legal actions resulted in $350 million in fines and mandatory restitution to affected clients.

Application of the 10 Habits to Mitigate Failures

1. Be Proactive: Anticipating Compliance Risks

Mitigation: Implementing regular risk assessments and proactive monitoring could have identified and addressed vulnerabilities before they escalated.

2. **Begin with Compliance by Design: Integrating Compliance into Processes**

Mitigation: Embedding compliance considerations into all product and service designs would have ensured adherence to regulations from inception.

3. **Put First Things First: Prioritizing Critical Compliance Issues**

Mitigation: Focusing on high-risk areas, such as AML controls and data protection, would have allocated resources effectively to prevent major breaches.

4. **Think Win-Win: Aligning Compliance with Business Objectives**

Mitigation: Aligning compliance strategies with business goals could have fostered a culture where ethical practices drive long-term profitability.

5. **Seek First to Understand: Grasping Regulatory Intent**

Mitigation: A deep understanding of the purpose behind the regulations would have guided the bank to implement measures that fulfill both the letter and spirit of the law.

6. **Synergize: Collaborating Across Functions**

Mitigation: Cross-departmental collaboration would have ensured that compliance is a shared responsibility, integrating insights from various functions to strengthen controls.

7. **Sharpen the Saw: Continuous Learning and Adaptation**

Mitigation: Ongoing training and staying abreast of regulatory changes would have equipped employees with the knowledge to adhere to compliance standards.

8. **Use Data as Your Compass: Data-Driven Compliance Monitoring**

Mitigation: Leveraging data analytics for real-time monitoring could have detected suspicious activities promptly, preventing large-scale violations.

9. **Build Culture: Fostering Integrity Over Enforcement**

Mitigation: Cultivating a culture that values ethical behavior over mere rule adherence would have encouraged employees to act responsibly without coercion.

10. **Lead Ethically: Exemplifying Integrity Beyond Compliance**

Mitigation: Leadership commitment to ethical practices would have set a tone from the top, influencing the entire organization to prioritize compliance.

Outcome

The absence of these ten habits at Global Trust Bank led to systemic compliance failures, resulting in substantial financial penalties and reputational harm. Had these principles been integrated into the bank's operations, many of the issues could have been identified and mitigated proactively, preserving the institution's integrity and standing in the financial community.

Part C- Quiz

1. Which habit emphasizes the importance of anticipating potential compliance issues before they arise?

a) Begin with Compliance by Design

b) Be Proactive

c) Synergize

d) Sharpen the Saw

2. Integrating compliance requirements into business processes from the outset refers to which habit?

a) Put First Things First

b) Begin with Compliance by Design

c) Think Win-Win

d) Seek First to Understand

3. Prioritizing critical compliance issues over less urgent matters aligns with which habit?

a) Put First Things First

b) Be Proactive

c) Use Data as Your Compass

d) Lead Ethically

4. Collaborating across various departments to address compliance challenges exemplifies which habit?

a) Synergize

b) Build Culture

c) Seek First to Understand

d) Think Win-Win

5. Continuously updating knowledge and skills in compliance reflects which habit?

a) Sharpen the Saw

b) Be Proactive

c) Use Data as Your Compass

d) Lead Ethically

6. Aligning compliance strategies with business objectives to benefit both parties is an example of which habit?

a) Think Win-Win

b) Synergize

c) Begin with Compliance by Design

d) Build Culture

7. Understanding the intent behind regulations before implementing compliance measures corresponds to which habit?

a) Seek First to Understand

b) Use Data as Your Compass

c) Put First Things First

d) Lead Ethically

8. Utilizing data analytics to monitor and guide compliance efforts pertains to which habit?

a) Use Data as Your Compass

b) Sharpen the Saw

c) Be Proactive

d) Synergize

9. Fostering an organizational environment where integrity is valued over mere rule enforcement is indicative of which habit?

a) Build Culture

b) Lead Ethically

c) Think Win-Win

d) Seek First to Understand

10. Demonstrating ethical behavior and setting a moral example within the organization aligns with which habit?

a) Lead Ethically

b) Build Culture

c) Be Proactive

d) Synergize

11. Which habit involves embedding compliance considerations into product and service development from the beginning?

a) Begin with Compliance by Design

b) Put First Things First

c) Seek First to Understand

d) Use Data as Your Compass

12. Regularly assessing and addressing potential compliance risks before they become issues is an aspect of which habit?

a) Be Proactive

b) Sharpen the Saw

c) Synergize

d) Think Win-Win

13. Encouraging open communication and collaboration between compliance and other departments exemplifies which habit?

a) Synergize

b) Build Culture

c) Seek First to Understand

d) Lead Ethically

14. Ensuring that compliance training and education are ongoing and up-to-date reflects which habit?

a) Sharpen the Saw

b) Be Proactive

c) Use Data as Your Compass

d) Begin with Compliance by Design

15. Balancing the needs of compliance with business goals to achieve mutual benefits is an example of which habit?

a) Think Win-Win

b) Synergize

c) Put First Things First

d) Seek First to Understand

16. Gaining a comprehensive understanding of regulatory requirements before acting corresponds to which habit?

a) Seek First to Understand

b) Use Data as Your Compass

c) Be Proactive

d) Lead Ethically

17. Leveraging technological tools to enhance compliance monitoring and decision-making pertains to which habit?

a) Use Data as Your Compass

b) Sharpen the Saw

c) Be Proactive

d) Synergize

18. Creating a workplace where ethical behavior is the norm and employees are encouraged to act with integrity aligns with which habit?

a) Build Culture

b) Lead Ethically

c) Think Win-Win

d) Seek First to Understand

19. Acting as a role model for ethical behavior and decision-making within the organization exemplifies which habit?

a) Lead Ethically

b) Build Culture

c) Be Proactive

d) Synergize

20. Addressing the most significant compliance risks before attending to less critical ones is an aspect of which habit?

a) Put First Things First

b) Begin with Compliance by Design

c) Seek First to Understand

d) Use Data as Your Compass

21. Collaborating with external partners and stakeholders to enhance compliance efforts is an example of which habit?

a) Synergize

b) Think Win-Win

c) Build Culture

d) Lead Ethically

22. Regularly reviewing and improving compliance policies and procedures to adapt to changing regulations reflects which habit?

a) Sharpen the Saw

b) Be Proactive

c) Use Data as Your Compass

d) Begin with Compliance by Design

23. Ensuring that compliance considerations are integrated into strategic planning processes pertains to which habit?

a) Begin with Compliance by Design

b) Put First Things First

c) Seek First to Understand

d) Think Win-Win

24. Promoting a culture where employees feel comfortable reporting compliance concerns, without fear of retaliation, aligns with which habit?

a) Build Culture

b) Lead Ethically

c) Synergize

d) Be Proactive

25. Utilizing key performance indicators (KPIs) to measure the effectiveness of compliance programs corresponds to which habit?

a) Use Data as Your Compass

b) Sharpen the Saw

c) Be Proactive

d) Think Win-Win

Answer Key:

1. b) Be Proactive

2. b) Begin with Compliance by Design

3. a) Put First Things First

4. a) Synergize

5. a) Sharpen the Saw

6. a) Think Win-Win

7. a) Seek First to Understand

8. a) Use Data as Your Compass

9. a) Build Culture

10. a) Lead Ethically

11. a) Begin with Compliance by Design

12. a) Be Proactive

13. a) Synergize

14. a) Sharpen the Saw

15. a) Think Win-Win

16. a) Seek First to Understand

17. a) Use Data as Your Compass

18. a) Build Culture

19. a) Lead Ethically

20. a) Put First Things First

21. a) Synergize

22. a) Sharpen the Saw

23. a) Begin with

24. b) Build Culture
25. b) Use Data as Your Compass

A. Templates & Checklists

Effective compliance programs rely on structured tools to ensure adherence to regulatory standards. Below are essential templates and checklists:

Compliance Risk Assessment Template

A structured tool designed to help organizations identify, evaluate, and prioritize compliance-related risks, ensuring alignment with legal and ethical standards.

Header	Description

Risk ID	Assign a unique identifier to each risk for easy tracking and reference.
Risk Category	Classify the risk into a specific category (e.g., Regulatory Compliance, Data Privacy, Financial Reporting) to facilitate organized analysis and management.
Risk Description	Provide a detailed explanation of the risk, including how it could potentially impact the organization. Clearly articulate the nature and context of the risk.
Legal/Regulatory Reference	Cite the specific laws, regulations, or standards related to the risk. This helps in understanding the compliance obligations and the potential consequences of non-compliance.
Likelihood of Occurrence	Assess and document the probability of the risk materializing. Common scales include Low, Medium, High. This evaluation aids in prioritizing risk management efforts.
Potential Impact	Evaluate the potential consequences if the risk were to occur. Consider factors such as financial loss, reputational damage, legal penalties, and operational disruption.
Risk Level/Priority	Determine the overall risk level by combining the likelihood and impact assessments. This can be represented using a risk matrix to categorize risks such as Low, Medium, High, or Extreme.
Existing Controls	List the current measures and controls in place to mitigate the risk. This includes policies, procedures, systems, and practices already implemented.
Control Effectiveness	Evaluate how effective the existing controls are in mitigating the risk. This assessment helps identify areas where controls may need enhancement.
Additional Mitigation Measures	Recommend further actions or controls required to reduce the risk to an acceptable level. This may involve introducing new policies, training programs, or technological solutions.

| Risk Owner | Assign responsibility for managing the risk to a specific individual or department. Clearly defining ownership ensures accountability and facilitates effective risk management. |
| Review Date | Specify the next scheduled date for reviewing the risk and the effectiveness of the mitigation measures. Regular reviews are essential to adapt to changing circumstances and ensure ongoing compliance. |

Compliance Audit Checklist

A comprehensive checklist outlining key elements of an effective compliance audit, including risk management practices, internal controls, and data security measures.

Header	Description
Audit Area	Specify the domain or function being audited (e.g., Data Privacy, Financial Reporting, Workplace Safety).
Compliance Requirement	Detail the specific legal, regulatory, or policy requirements applicable to the audit area.
Audit Question/Check	Pose a clear question or statement to assess compliance with the specified requirement.
Findings	Document observations and evidence collected during the audit related to the compliance check.

Compliance Status	Indicate whether the requirement is: Compliant, Non-Compliant, or Not Applicable.
Risk Level	Assess the potential impact of non-compliance as Low, Medium, or High.
Recommendations	Provide suggested corrective actions or improvements to address any identified non-compliance issues.
Responsible Party	Assign the individual or department accountable for implementing the recommended actions.
Target Completion Date	Set a deadline for completing the corrective actions.
Status Updates	Track progress on implementing recommendations, noting dates and details of updates.

Self-Assessment Checklist

An extensive checklist of compliance practices found in industry-leading programs, allowing companies to confidentially assess their progress and prioritize improvement efforts.

B. Self-Assessment Summary Across All Habits

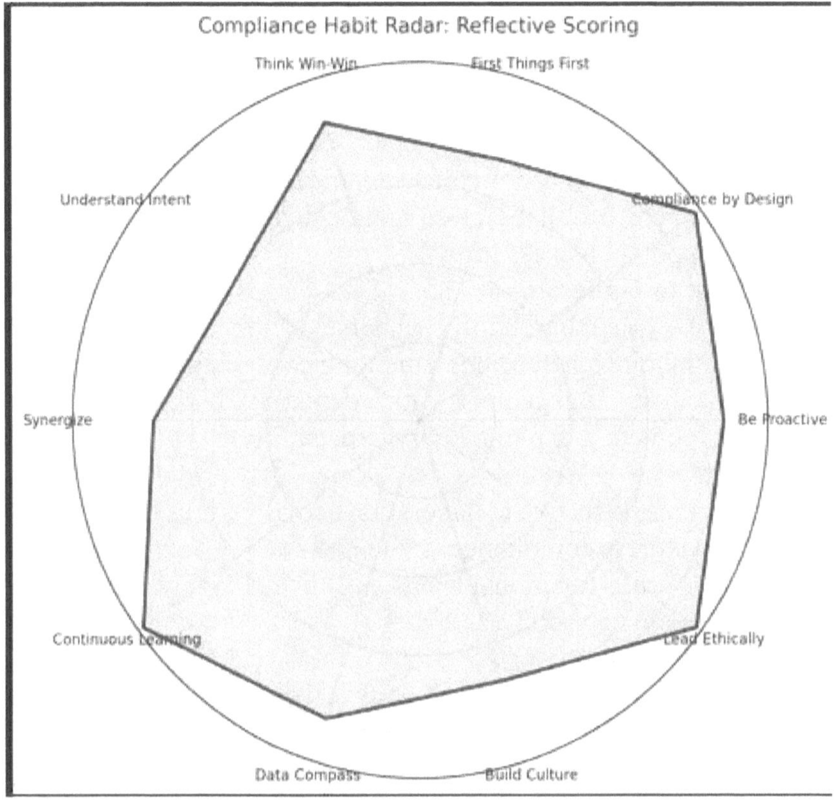

To evaluate proficiency in the "10 Habits of Effective Compliance Professionals," the following self-assessment summary is provided:

1. **Be Proactive**
   - Do you regularly conduct risk assessments to anticipate potential compliance issues?
   - Are proactive measures in place to address identified risks before they escalate?
2. **Begin with Compliance by Design**
   - Is compliance integrated into the initial stages of product and service development?
   - Are compliance considerations embedded into business processes from the outset?
3. **Put First Things First**

- o Are critical compliance issues prioritized over less urgent matters?
  - o Is there an effective allocation of resources to address high-risk areas promptly?

4. **Think Win-Win**
   - o Are compliance strategies aligned with business objectives to benefit all stakeholders?
   - o Is there a collaborative approach to ensure compliance supports business growth?

5. **Seek First to Understand**
   - o Do you thoroughly understand the intent behind regulations before implementing compliance measures?
   - o Is there engagement with regulatory bodies and legal experts to grasp regulatory expectations?

6. **Synergize**
   - o Is there effective collaboration across various departments to address compliance challenges?
   - o Are cross-functional teams established to develop holistic compliance solutions?

7. **Sharpen the Saw**
   - o Do you engage in continuous learning to stay updated on emerging compliance trends and regulations?
   - o Are there regular training programs to enhance compliance knowledge and skills?

8. **Use Data as Your Compass**
   - o Are data analytics utilized to monitor and guide compliance efforts effectively?
   - o Are data-driven insights employed to detect and prevent compliance violations?

9. **Build Culture**
   - o Is there a culture that values integrity and ethical behavior over mere rule enforcement?
   - o Are employees encouraged to internalize compliance values and act accordingly?

10. **Lead Ethically**
    - o Do leaders exemplify ethical behavior and set a moral example within the organization?
    - o Is there transparency and accountability in decision-making processes?

C. Glossary of Key Compliance Terms

- **Compliance**

  Adherence to laws, regulations, guidelines, and specifications relevant to an organization's business.

- **Risk Management**

  The process of identifying, assessing, and controlling threats to an organization's capital and earnings.

  Due Diligence

  An investigation or audit of a potential investment or product to confirm all facts, such as reviewing financial records.

- **Internal Controls**

  Processes implemented to provide assurance regarding the effectiveness and efficiency of operations, reliability of financial reporting, and compliance with laws and regulations.

- **Code of Conduct**

A set of principles and expectations that are considered binding on any person who is a member of a particular group.

- **Audit**

An official inspection of an organization's accounts, typically by an independent body.

- **Bribe**

Something that is given or offered to a person or organization to encourage that person/organization to take an action of benefit to the giver.

- **Governance**

The system by which organizations are directed and controlled, encompassing the mechanisms, processes, and relations by which corporations are controlled and operated.

- **Fraud**

Wrongful or criminal deception intended to result in financial or personal gain.

- **Transparency**

The quality of being done in an open way without secrets.

9 798899 294303